Questions Literacy Resources

The Story of Tracy Beaker

Compiled by Liz Ross

Activities and teachers' notes
based on the novel by Jacqueline Wilson

THE QUESTIONS PUBLISHING COMPANY LTD

BIRMINGHAM

2000

First published in 2000 by
The Questions Publishing Company Ltd
27 Frederick Street, Birmingham B1 3HH

Designed by Al Stewart
Edited by Diane Parkin
Cover design by John Minnett

ISBN: 1-84190-030-3

Also available from the The Questions Publishing Company Ltd:

Questions Literacy Resources

Bill's New Frock
based on the novel by Anne Fine and compiled by Marian Dean

Contents

Introduction and teachers' notes

Part 1: Activities

Activity 1: My autobiography

Activity 2: Debate on education

Activity 3: If I won a million pounds…

Activity 4: Tracy's opinions

Activity 5: Is it always wrong to hit someone?

Activity 6: Creative writing: exaggeration

Activity 7: Persuasive arguments

Activity 8: Feeling hurt

Activity 9: Cloze activity

Activity 10: Nightmare

Activity 11: A play

Activity 12: Report on Tracy Beaker

Activity 13: Looks

Activity 14: Suitable clothes?

Activity 15: Reading survey

Activity 16: Throwing a wobbly

Activity 17: Dares

Activity 18: Handwriting

Activity 19: An alternative fairy tale

Activity 20: Bullying

Activity 21: First day nerves

Activity 22: Conflicts

Activity 23: Sequence the story

Part 2: Activities for the whole book

Activity 24: Continuing The Story of Tracy Beaker

Activity 25: Crossword

Activity 26: Design your own crossword

Activity 27: Spelling sheets

Activity 28: Tracy Beaker – my review

Activity 29: Target readers

Activity 30: Comparing books by the same author

Introduction and teachers' notes

This pack was written in the hope of easing the workload of busy, stressed teachers (are there any other types?) It does not include copious teachers' notes (you could probably use the pack without reading the notes at all) but I would advise reading them beforehand, if at all possible.

The pack contains worksheets and activity ideas based on an excellent book: *The Story of Tracy Beaker* by Jacqueline Wilson. I feel that it particularly appeals to less able or less motivated readers and, because of Tracy's character, to pupils with behavioural problems. I trialled the pack on a year 6 class with a high proportion of such pupils, and I think it worked very well. I remember one pupil whose motivation was particularly poor, saying to me after several lessons: "That's more work than I've done in the whole of my school life!"

The pack can be used within the Literacy Hour for shared reading sessions, followed by word, sentence or text-level work (the activities are labelled as such).

There are also some cross-curricular elements, as follows:

Activity 4 incorporates some art and history work;
Activities 14 and 15 include some design and technology work;
Activity 15 also includes some maths work;
Activity 24 contains history work.

It is difficult to generalise about which age-group this pack would suit, but I would say roughly years 4 to 9, as the main character is ten years old.

This pack is in two parts. The first part consists of a set of activities based on a few pages of reading that could be done at the beginning of each lesson. The second part contains activities based on the overall book, to help the pupils gain a sense of the book as a whole.

Each text extract has a main activity (aimed at the majority of the class) and a prompt sheet, providing a simpler activity structure (and requiring less writing) for those who need it. Finally, there are extension activities for those who finish the main activity quickly and may need stretching.

It is worth reading the following teachers' notes before attempting the activities. The notes for activities 5, 7, 11, 13, 16, 17, 19, 20, 28, 29 and 30 should be looked at a week or so in advance of the lesson, rather than the night before, which would be fine for the others.

Activity 1

I feel that it is important, with this activity, to emphasise that pupils shouldn't make negative comments about people who can't defend themselves. If they do need to write negative comments, they should at least change people's names.

Bear in mind that some pupils may not want to disclose all of the personal details required by the task.
If you have pupils who are likely to get to the extension activities, you will need to have television listings ready.

Activity 2

You may want to think about your groupings beforehand and go over the ground rules for group work. Ensure that everyone in the group:

- has a chance to tell the rest of the group their ideas;
- listens when someone else is speaking;
- accepts what someone has said, stating their views as positively as possible;
- doesn't always expect to have their ideas supported by the rest of the group;
- agrees to disagree if the group can't decide on a particular issue.

Again, it is important to emphasise that negative comments should be avoided, particularly about members of staff.

If you are planning to send the ideas to the LEA, it may be an idea to have a large envelope, already addressed, to put them in at the end of the lesson.

Activity 4

I have come across a lot of pupils of various ages, who have problems putting themselves in other people's shoes, and find the task of writing from someone else's viewpoint difficult. A fun way of introducing this might be to get the pupils to imagine what inanimate objects would say if they could talk.

For example:

An expensive shoe in a shoe shop that has been tried on many times, but not bought, may complain to the other shoes. If it were stuck in a box most of the time, shoved on people's smelly feet, and never cleaned, then it couldn't be expected to be at its best – and the customers in this particular shop have no taste anyway! (etc.)

Other ideas could include: deckchairs; chairs; cars; toys; balls; sports equipment; Christmas trees; vegetables; etc.

The extension activity demonstrates the difference between **fact** and **opinion**, which is an important objective for a history lesson. You may want to do some follow-up history work on this subject.

You will need plain paper for anyone doing the art extension activity.

Activity 5

As with Activity 2, you may want to remind pupils about the ground rules for group work and think about your groupings.

It may be appropriate to do some role-play with the pupils in this lesson, on the theme of dealing with problems in a non-violent manner. I found the publication *Bullying: don't suffer in silence*, by the Department for Education (1994) useful: although mainly to do with bullying, it has a very good section on asserting yourself without violence.

You could develop the extension activity into a class debate on banning boxing.

Activity 7

It would be helpful if you could watch the film *Twelve Angry Men*, starring Henry Fonda, or take the pupils to a court hearing as a follow-up to this activity.

Activity 8

Again, re-emphasise the point about avoiding negative comments, and/or changing names.

You may also feel that it is important to point out to the pupils that putting a case reasonably is **always** a better option.

Activity 9

If you have pupils who are likely to do the extension activities, you will need to have a thesaurus (or several) handy, as well as dictionaries.

Activity 10

You may want to ask the pupils to write on alternate lines, as this makes it much easier for marking and re-drafting.

If you have pupils who have problems identifying or using adjectives, you may want to do some revision or introductory work on adjectives, and perhaps nouns, before attempting this activity. Alternatively, you could do the extension activity first.

Activity 11

You could have another actor read out the directions, and these pupils could direct the acting if the group goes on to do the extension activity.

It would be useful to have a red lipstick for the actors to pretend to use (for hygiene) if they are doing the extension activity.

For those pupils doing the extension activity, stress that there shouldn't be any physical contact.

Activity 13

If you have pupils who are likely to be doing the extension activity, you may want to decide beforehand which advertising companies the pupils could send their ideas to, and have addresses and envelopes ready.

It may be appropriate here to do some role-play work or have a follow-up discussion on: 'Feeling good about the person inside' or: 'Everyone has the right to feel good about themselves'.

Activity 16

It may be useful to do some introductory, revision or follow-up work on writing in different tenses here.

You may also want to think about having appropriate literature available for the pupils to use, when doing the extension activity.

Activity 17

You may feel that it is appropriate to do a role-play or a discussion about the extension activity topic of peer pressure, and how to resist it.

Activity 18

For these handwriting activities, it is important to remind pupils of the necessary preparation, before starting:

If you are writing with a pencil, make sure that it is long enough to hold properly and that it is sharp;
Make sure, if you are left-handed, that you sit on the left side of right-handers;

Sit comfortably and squarely in front of your desk.

Activity 19

You may want to try and get hold of a copy of *There's a Wolf in My Pudding*, as mentioned on the worksheet.

You may also want to discuss elements of a good story with the pupils (from the extension sheet) before writing.

As mentioned before, it makes it a lot easier to redraft and mark if the pupils write on alternate lines.

You may also want to talk about different ways of planning a story before this lesson: a suggested story plan could be as follows:

Beginning

WHO is in the story? (Characters and character descriptions.)
WHERE is it set? (You need to be specific about where it is set. It may be a different country or a parallel world.)
WHEN is it set? (Is it in the past, present or future? How far into the past or future?)

Middle

WHAT happens? (An exciting event? Is there a problem to be solved?)
WHAT else happens? (Try to extend your story with at least *one* other exciting event.)
WHY do characters do what they do? What is their motivation?

Ending

HAPPY?
SAD?
CLIFFHANGER? (This is the trickiest of the three to do well. Think of the way that 'soap' episodes always end. There's usually a dramatic event, and the programme finishes as you're about to learn exactly what the ending is, or how people will react. You're left 'hanging off the edge of a cliff', i.e. in suspense.)

Activity 20

You may feel it is appropriate to do some follow-up work on bullying here.

Activity 21

As mentioned, writing on alternate lines makes the work easier to re-draft and mark.

You may want to do some revision or follow-up work on adverbs, and perhaps verbs. Alternatively, you could do the extension activity first.

Activity 23

The correct sequence of events on the main worksheet is as follows:

Tracy's mum, whom she adores, leaves her.
Tracy is fostered by Aunty Peggy.
Tracy goes to her first children's home and meets baby Camilla.
Tracy is fostered by Julie and Ted.
Tracy makes friends with Louise at her second children's home.
Justine arrives at her second children's home.
Tracy falls out with Justine and Louise.
Tracy meets Cam.
Peter meets a couple who want to foster him.
Tracy makes up with Justine.

* Emphasise that the above statements are story *facts* and the comments they add beneath them are *opinions*. You may want to do some follow-up history work on this.

Activity 24

It would be useful to have at least a few copies of a page of the play script in Activity 11 here.

Activity 25

The answers to the crossword are below:

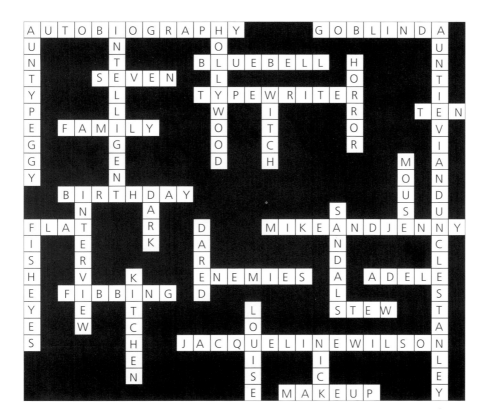

The answers to the prompt crossword are below:

Activity 26

It would be useful to have a lot of large squared paper for this activity.

Activity 27

Here are five sets of words that appear in the book. In each set there are three lists of ten words. List A contains the more common, everyday words. List B contains more unusual words. List C contains the most complex words.

The first few words in each list of the set have a spelling rule in common.

Choose the list appropriate to the pupil. If ten words are too many to learn, give them a few from the list and, similarly, if ten are too few, give them a few more from the next list.

Because it is important to teach spellings within a context, each set of words comes with a matching set of sentences. This means that the spellings can be read to the pupils in context and you can read the sentences to the pupils again when you test them, so they are spelt within a context.

I have found (and other teachers seem to agree) that one of the best ways of learning spellings is to: **look**, **cover**, **write** and **check**. This literally means, look at the word carefully and think about the sounds. Then cover the word and attempt to write it from memory. Next, uncover your attempt and check it against the original. I usually ask the pupils if they can get it right five times.

Activity 28

You may want to have other books the pupils have read available for this lesson.

Activity 29

You may want to have a wide range of books available here.

Activity 30

You may want to have several books by an author or authors available here. If you want to use some other Jacqueline Wilson books, I would recommend *Double Act* and *The Bed and Breakfast Star*.

Part 1: Activities

Activity 1

My autobiography

Read to page 23.

Tracy tells you about herself.

⭢ Start your autobiography in the same way. Answer these questions in sentences. Separate your writing into paragraphs as shown.

☆ Where and when were you born? Was there anything memorable about your birth? Not that you would remember yourself, but something someone told you about it. If you could have another nationality, what would it be and why?

☆ Do you have a lucky number/charm/piece of clothing? Why is it lucky for you? Think of a few things that have happened to you that were unlucky and/or lucky. Maybe you have nearly had a serious accident.

☆ Who do you consider to be your closest friend/friends? What do you think are the most important things about a good friend? Perhaps it's that you can trust them. They're fun to be with, they listen well, they help you. You may have similar interests.

☆ Which foods do you enjoy most? If you could have a year's free supply of any food, what would it be? What is the healthiest three-course meal you would eat and what is the most unhealthy you would eat?

☆ Do you have a pet? Do you have any stories to recount about them? For example, worst/best moments. If you were to choose an unusual pet, what would it be?

☆ What are your favourite television programmes and films or videos?

☆ What sorts of things do you really hate? The things I hate include biting into a piece of foil by accident, and my husband ignoring me when he's watching the football.

☆ Who do you live with? With which members of your family do you get on best? Recount one of your most memorable moments with your family. Do you have a large family? In which parts of the world do you have relatives?

Note: Try not to make negative comments about people and/or change names.

Extension activities

1. Talking of favourite foods and health, write down what you would say to someone who asked you if you thought you were healthy and why.

2. On the subject of an unusual pet, imagine the kind of problems you could have with it and write a story about it.

3. Tracy talks about her favourite TV programmes. Plan a day's scheduling on a new television channel from seven o'clock in the morning to ten o'clock at night. Try to balance the programmes so that they appeal to as many people as possible. Look at a TV guide to help you if you have one.

Activity 1 – prompt sheet

My autobiography

I was born in _____

One of the first things I remember as a baby was _____

If I could live in another country it would be _____

I have a lucky _____

One of the luckiest things that has happened to me was _____

_____

I consider my closest friend/s to be _____

I think a good friend is someone who _____

_____

My favourite food is _____

The *healthiest* three-course meal I would eat is:

Starter _____

Main course _____

Dessert _____

I have a pet _____ If I could have a very unusual pet it would be a

_____

The things I hate are _____

_____

Of my family I get on best with _____

I have family living in the following towns/countries _____

_____

Activity 2

Debate on education

Read pages 20 and 21.

Tracy talks about her school.

⊃ In groups of two or four make a list of some of the best and worst things about school. No negative comments about staff, please!

⊃ Now plan a package of improvements in the education system. Issues to consider include the following:

☆ Class sizes – should there be a maximum or minimum number?
☆ Single sex education – which subjects?
☆ Support teachers in the classroom – should every class have one? Should there be a maximum number of teachers in a classroom?
☆ Special needs schools – should there be more special needs schools or more integration of pupils with special educational needs into the 'normal' classroom?
☆ When and in what form should pupils be assessed? At what ages should pupils be assessed or take exams? Which is better – continual assessment or exams?
☆ Uniform – should all pupils wear uniforms? What sorts of clothes should the uniform allow?
☆ Discipline – how should school and classroom rules be decided on and enforced?
☆ School meals – what sort of menus and systems of payment do you think there should be?
☆ School days – would you start the school day earlier or later? Would you rather come to school for some of the weekend in place of some weekday times? Would you re-arrange the school holidays?
☆ Any other issue you consider important.

⊃ Present your ideas to the class.

Extension activity

Summarise your ideas in a letter to the education authority. Remember to explain who you are and how you arrived at these ideas. Try to write persuasively, anticipating any immediate concerns they may have, if you can.

Activity 2 – prompt sheet

Debate on education

We decided that class sizes should be _____

We think that single sex education is/is not a good idea because _____

_____

We agreed that there should be *one/two/three/more* support teachers in each

classroom providing help.

We think that there should be *more/less* special needs schools.

On the issue of assessment we decided that

_____

_____

The school uniform should be

_____

_____

We decided that school rules should be

_____

_____

We would like school meals to be

_____

_____

We would/wouldn't change school days and holidays (to)

_____

_____

Activity 3

If I won a million pounds . . .

Read page 23.

Tracy thinks about what she would do if she were rich.

⊃ If you won one million pounds on the lottery, and you couldn't spend more than £100,000 on one sort of thing, i.e. if you had to buy *at least* ten things all under £100,000, how would you spend it?

Extension activity

Write a letter to a friend describing in detail how you're enjoying spending the money, what you've done with it and what your life is like now. (Something to think about: do you think coming into a lot of money would always change people's lives for the better?)

Activity 3 – prompt sheet

If I won a million pounds . . .

If I were to win one million pounds on the lottery and I had to buy at least ten things all under £100,000, they would be:

_____

_____

_____

_____

_____

_____

_____

_____

_____

_____

_____

_____

_____

Things you might choose from: house; castle; stately home; swimming pool; employ people to look after you and your property; speed boat; yacht; house boat; caravan; a holiday; a particular company/set up in business; a plot of land to build something on; antiques; car; gym equipment; jet/aeroplane; helicopter.

Alternatively you might want to learn a new and expensive activity, i.e. skiing; run for office; give to charities and/or family and friends.

Activity 4

Tracy's opinions

Read pages 24 – 39.

You learn more about Tracy and her relationships with the other people in her life: Aunty Peggy; Elaine; Peter; Jenny; Louise; and Justine.

⊃ If *Tracy* were to describe each of these people in a short paragraph, what would she say about them? Remember to use Tracy's terminology.

To help you I've listed the pages that tell you what Tracy thinks of each person. The pages in brackets only give you a little information about the person.

Aunty Peggy: p. 25 – 26 (p 34).

Elaine: p. 27 – 30.

Peter Ingham: p. 30 – 32.

Jenny: (p 33) p. 37 – 38.

Justine: (p 31) p. 34 – 37.

Louise: p. 34 – 35.

Extension activity

Imagine you are Tracy's social worker and write down how you would attempt to help Tracy to get on more with the people she comes across. What would you say to her? Perhaps you would set up role-playing situations for her.

Activity 4 – prompt sheet

Tracy's opinions

Dear Diary,

Let me tell you about some of the people I have come across in my life:

Aunty Peggy is

_____

_____

Elaine is

_____

_____

Peter Ingham is

_____

_____

_____

Jenny is

_____

_____

Justine is

_____

_____

_____

Louise is

_____

_____

Activity 5

Is it always wrong to hit someone?

Read page 26.

You learn that Aunty Peggy used to smack Tracy.

⊃ Debate, as a class, whether you think it is always wrong to hit someone.

Consider, first, parents hitting their children. Issues to consider include:

☆ Are there degrees of hitting? Is a smack with the hand the same as a smack with an object?
☆ Does it depend on which part of the body is struck?
☆ Does violence breed violence?
☆ Are there alternative methods of discipline?
☆ How could it be controlled? Should it be up to the parents and no-one else?
☆ Would you smack your kids?

Now consider the issues around corporal punishment being re-introduced into schools:

☆ What form would the punishment take? Slipper? Cane? Hand?
☆ For what reasons should pupils be punished? I always remember being given the slipper when I was about ten in front of a class of six-year-olds, for going on the mud when I'd been told not to. The worst thing about it was that I had no intention of going on the mud, but someone had pushed me.
☆ How could it be controlled in schools? Parental consent?
☆ Who would administer the punishment? Only the headteacher? Teachers may not be willing to administer it.

What about hitting another person you have a problem with?

☆ How else could you resolve the problem?
☆ Are there certain situations that justify hitting someone?
☆ Does it depend on whether the person is younger or older than you? What if they are smaller or bigger than you? What if they were younger but bigger than you, or older but smaller?

My own personal view is that when you hit someone you often forget about the mental as well as physical damage you are doing. You should ask yourself whether you feel you have the right to inflict this on them. Apart from this, fighting usually gets you into trouble. If you have a problem with someone, you should be strong enough to try everything you can to sort it out reasonably. If that fails you should be strong enough to walk away and try to forget it. If you can do this you have won. You have proved yourself stronger (whether others think so or not) because it is much harder to walk away.

Extension activity

Prepare a speech for the Boxing Association either for or against the motion that boxing should be banned. First, think of these issues:

☆ What sorts of dangers are there in boxing? Consider three facts. Fact one – every time someone is hit hard on the head their brain is damaged to some extent because it comes into contact with the skull. Fact two – people have died while boxing. Fact three – there are a lot of injuries and deaths in other sports too.

☆ Does boxing provide an alternative for people who might otherwise be violent outside the gym, or does it teach them to be violent?

☆ Are there improvements that could be made in order to make boxing more acceptable? For example, having doctors on hand, wearing more protective gear, shorter fights, etc.

☆ What would happen if boxing were banned?

Activity 5 – prompt sheet

Is it always wrong to hit someone?

Firstly we considered parents or carers hitting children. We think that

_____

_____

_____

Next we discussed corporal punishment in schools. We decided that

_____

_____

_____

When it comes to hitting someone you have a problem with, we think that

_____

_____

_____

Activity 6

Creative writing: exaggeration

Read pages 40 – 45.

On pages 40 – 42, Tracy exaggerates about her trip to town. What she actually did was '. . . loaf around town feeling more and more fed up'. However, before she admits this she tells us a story of an amazing time in town, describing lunch at McDonald's, then a really funny film at a cinema, a winning streak on the fruit machines and a great party where one of her friends invited her to live in her house.

We often exaggerate about things that have happened to us to make them sound more interesting.

⊃ Choose at least one of the following situations and write a more detailed, exaggerated version:

☆ A Saturday in town when you wandered around the shops with a friend or friends;
☆ A trip to a concert to see a band;
☆ A visit to a sports centre or gym;
☆ A trip to a football match;
☆ Your witnessing the police talking to a neighbour;
☆ Your witnessing a man being chased down the street.

Alternatively you could use a situation of your own choosing.

Extension activity

List the most exaggerated excuses you can think of for not being able to hand your homework in.

Activity 6 – prompt sheet

Creative writing: exaggeration

When you are in town you could say that you spent lots of money on things you wanted like food and clothes. Perhaps you saw a celebrity shopping and got their autograph and went for a drink with them. You might have been asked to do some market research on something secret or strange and got some 'freebies'. Perhaps you saw some thieves stealing from a shop and being chased by security guards.

⊃ You could begin with: 'I was wandering around town on Saturday . . .'

A trip to a concert might include things like fireworks, lasers and smoke. You may have had front row seats and/or got up on stage. What about going backstage after the concert and meeting the band or singer, and them inviting you to the after-show party where you learn all about them? Perhaps they take you for a drive in their limousine.*

⊃ You could begin with: 'I went to a fantastic concert . . .'

A visit to a sports centre or gym might include you doing amazingly well in a match or on the gym equipment. Perhaps you meet a sporting celebrity there and he or she teaches you a few things or you beat him or her at something.

⊃ You could begin with: 'When I went to the gym . . .' or 'I went to the sports centre to play . . .'

A trip to a football match might include your team playing amazing football with a huge score line. Maybe you could say there were so many there that some were turned away. Perhaps the ball flew into the stands and you caught it. Maybe you were asked to be ball-person at the last minute. You could have sneaked into the dressing room and heard the team talk and/or met the players and got their autographs. Perhaps you were the mascot for the match. You could have been asked to make the announcements during the match.

⊃ You could begin with: 'I had a fantastic time at the football match ...'

Your seeing the police talk to your neighbour could turn out to be the start of an investigation into a multi-million pound fraud. Perhaps they sent some money away to a bogus company that then disappeared. Maybe you do some detecting of your own and manage to track the villains down after a long chase.

⊃ You could begin with: 'I saw the police talking to my neighbour. It turned out that . . .'

Your seeing a man being chased down the street could be the beginning of a very long and dangerous pursuit. You could follow and see the man and his pursuer/s jump over fences, run across roads, try to get away in a car, jump off roofs or bridges, swim across a river and try to hide in his attempt to get away. It may be that he was a plain clothes detective being pursued by villains or that the villain was being pursued by the police.

⊃ You could begin with: 'The man sprinted down the street. He was being chased by . . .'

*Note: Of course, in real life, an adult should know where you are at *all* times

Activity 7

Persuasive arguments

On pages 43 – 44.

Tracy uses her imagination to think of some good arguments in her own defence concerning the clock incident. She admits to being in Justine's room and to looking at the clock. Then she goes on to say that she didn't intend to break it and was only going to look at it. She argues that Louise had told her it was 'special' and it should therefore have stood up to a bit of twiddling. Another of her arguments is that it was very likely to have fallen apart the next time Justine touched it.

Imagine that you are a lawyer. You are defending a client who has been charged with the theft of an antique clock. You will have to use a lot of imagination as the evidence against him is considerable:

☆ Your client's fingerprints are all over the room;
☆ He eats Mars Bars all the time and a wrapper was found after the burglary;
☆ The victim came downstairs with a torch and scared the burglar away but he saw that he or she was wearing black jeans and a black leather jacket with writing on it, both of which your client owns;
☆ Your client has been in the victim's house before, when he was doing some work there, and could have seen the clock.

About your client:

☆ He is 18 and works as an electrician's assistant;
☆ He has several burglary convictions in the past but has not been in trouble with the police for three years;
☆ On the night of the burglary he says he was visiting his disabled mum;
☆ His mum says that he was with her;
☆ He swears that he doesn't know anything about antiques.

⊃ Write out your speech to the jury. Remember that all you have to do is put reasonable doubt in their minds that your client is guilty. You should tackle it in three ways:

☆ Persuade them that the evidence doesn't point conclusively to your client, e.g. if your client likes Mars Bars and there's a wrapper at the scene of the crime, does that prove he did it?
☆ Offer alternative explanations for the evidence, e.g. maybe the victim took the clock himself to claim the insurance;
☆ Try to get the jury to sympathise with your client, e.g. your client has been looking after his disabled mum.

Extension activity

Write a similar speech as the defence lawyer for the big bad wolf in the story of Little Red Riding Hood. You may change the fairy tale a little if you like. You need to present your client as a much misunderstood creature who wouldn't dream of eating Granny. Perhaps you admit to your client being in the wood and say he was starving, but was only after the picnic basket. Perhaps there were other wolves in the wood at the time. Perhaps he was wearing Granny's clothes for a laugh or a dare.

Activity 7 – prompt sheet

Persuasive arguments

Your Honour, learned colleagues, members of the jury, ladies and gentlemen, I am here to convince you that the prosecution has not got conclusive evidence that my client stole the clock because he didn't.

My client is a good man. He has a good job as

_____

_____

On the night of the burglary he

_____

_____

My client did not steal the antique clock because

_____

_____

The evidence the police have is not conclusive. My client's fingerprints could be all over the room because

_____

_____

Yes, my client eats Mars Bars, but

_____

_____

Yes, my client owns a black leather jacket with writing on it, but

_____

_____

I conclude that you can't be sure, beyond a reasonable doubt, that my client did it and you must then find him innocent.

Activity 8

Feeling hurt

Read pages 46 – 51.

You learn about the breakdown of Tracy's second placement with Julie and Ted.

Tracy obviously feels hurt that Julie and Ted could dump her that way.

⊃ Imagine that *you* are Tracy and write a letter to Julie and Ted telling them how you feel about the situation. You might want to include some of the following things:

☆ How Tracy hadn't been sure of them at first and then had come to be very fond of them – especially after her first placement with Aunty Peggy;
☆ How she had begun to imagine staying with them until her mum came for her;
☆ How she had been hurt that they didn't want her any more when they knew they were having their own baby;
☆ How she can't understand why they couldn't have been a family together;
☆ How she would have cared for the baby and that she wouldn't have treated it like she had done baby Stephen.

Try to use Tracy's terminology.

Alternatively you could imagine or recall a situation where someone hurt you. Write a letter to this person explaining exactly how you felt about it. Explain things reasonably. If you are abusive it won't help. Try not to be too negative about people.

Extension activity

Write another short letter back from Julie and Ted explaining their feelings.

Activity 8 – prompt sheet

Feeling hurt

Put your address on the first four lines, the date on the fifth and then complete the sentences.

_____

_____

_____

_____

_____

Dear Julie and Ted,

I felt that I had to write to you. There are some things I need to say to you. I was really unhappy at my first placement with that nasty old Aunty Peggy, so I wasn't sure about you at first.

I don't find it easy to trust people but you were so nice to me that after a while I

_____

I hoped that I could stay with you while I waited for

_____

I thought we were all so happy. Why did it all change when you found out

_____

Why couldn't we have been one big happy family? Were you worried about how I would be with the new baby? You didn't need to be. Your baby would be much nicer than that little monster baby Stephen. I would be great with the new baby. I would

_____

I am angry that you have dumped me.

Yours sincerely

_____

Activity 9

Cloze activity

The passage below is taken from the book, pages 49 – 50.

Tracy is trying to convince Elaine that she would be great with Julie's baby.

Copy the passage below into your book, under the title 'Cloze' and put the word in each gap that you think is most appropriate. Don't refer to the book until you have finished.

"So why can't I go on living with them? Look, I'll help all I can. Julie doesn't need

to _____. I'll be just like a second mum to this baby. I know all what to

do. I can give it its bottle and change its soggy old _____ and thump it

on its _____ to bring up its wind.

"I'm dead _____ where babies are concerned."

"Yes, I know, Tracy. But that's just the _____. You see when Julie

and Ted first _____ you, we did tell them a bit about your

_____ and the trouble you had in your first foster home. You know, when

you shut the baby up in the _____."

"That was Steve. And he wasn't a baby. He was a _____ little

toddler, and he kept _____ up our bedroom so I tidied him up into the

cupboard just for a bit so I could get everything _____ out."

"And there was the ghost game that got _____ out of hand."

"Oh that! All those kids _____ that game. I was ever so good at

_____ the right hiding places and then I'd start an eerie sort of

_____ and then I'd jump out at them, _____ this old white sheet."

"And everyone got _____ silly."

"No they didn't. They just squealed because they were excited."

Extension activity

You may have used words other than the one in the book, but with the same meaning.

Write another sentence for each of the following words, using a dictionary if you need to.

☆ trouble   ☆ foul
☆ total   ☆ love
☆ scare

Now look these words up in a thesaurus to find different words with the same meaning, i.e. **synonyms**, and write them out.

Activity 9 – prompt sheet

Cloze activity

"So why can't I go on living with them? Look, I'll help all I can. Julie doesn't need

to _____. I'll be just like a second mum to this baby. I know all what to

do. I can give it its bottle and change its soggy old _____ and thump it

on its _____ to bring up its wind.

   "I'm dead _____ where babies are concerned."

   "Yes, I know, Tracy. But that's just the _____. You see when Julie

and Ted first _____ you, we did tell them a bit about your

_____ and the trouble you had in your first foster home. You know, when

you shut the baby up in the _____."

   "That was Steve. And he wasn't a baby. He was a _____ little

toddler, and he kept _____ up our bedroom so I tidied him up into the

cupboard just for a bit so I could get everything _____ out."

   "And there was the ghost game that got _____ out of hand."

   "Oh that! All those kids _____ that game. I was ever so good at

_____ the right hiding places and then I'd start an eerie sort of

_____ and then I'd jump out at them, _____ this old white sheet."

   "And everyone got _____ silly."

   "No they didn't. They just squealed because they were excited."

The missing words are listed below but sometimes there are two words with similar
meanings, i.e. **synonyms**, that you must choose between (in italics):

back; *trouble/problem*; *history/background*; *nasty/foul*; *straightened/sorted*;

adored/loved; *noise/moan*; *frightened/scared*; *panic/worry*; nappy; experienced;

fostered; cupboard; *messing/mucking*; *totally/completely*; finding; wearing.

Activity 10

Nightmare

Read from page 52, up to and including the first paragraph on page 59.

On pages 57 – 58 Tracy tells you about one of her nightmares.

A lot of people have nightmares or strange dreams although sometimes it's hard to remember them when you wake up. Some people believe that dreams are the result of your mind trying to clear out some of your old thoughts or worries. I always used to dream of being chased by something or someone and, no matter how hard I tried, I could never run away. I've had several really strange dreams but there was one nightmare I used to get all the time: I would be walking near a railway track and I would see a friend walking across it towards me.

Suddenly a train would come out of nowhere and knock my friend down. I would rush over to her. The train would stop and I would pick my friend up and carry her to the train. I would be crying and yelling at the driver and as he opened the doors I would climb on board to see that the passengers were all skeletons and zombies. They all laughed at me as the doors closed. I would always wake up at this point, often crying. I always seem to wake from nightmares just before I'm going to be killed.

➲ Discuss as a class the sort of dreams you have. Do you, or does anyone you know, sleepwalk? What do you think particular dreams mean?

Nightmares can be used as the basis for good horror stories.

➲ Write a horror story based on your nightmares, or mine, or just on what scares you. Writing on alternate lines will make it easier to re-draft you story. Add your own title when you've finished your story.

Extension activity

Re-draft your story concentrating on your adjectives so that your story is both more scary and more vivid.

Do this quick exercise on adjectives first to remind you what they are.

An adjective tells you more about a noun, i.e. a person, place or thing. Underline the adjectives in the story. The first two are done for you. Find the other ten.

The <u>big</u>, <u>hairy</u> gorilla stared at the horrible little boy who was making faces at it through the window of its small enclosure. It sat there for a minute and then, just as the foul boy had run out of ideas, it charged at the thick, plastic window and thumped it with its fists and let out a fierce, ear-piercing noise. The boy dissolved into a screaming, hysterical coward and ran for his mother. The gorilla went back to his place, smiling to himself.

Insert a second, appropriate adjective into the space on each line of this list poem about food:

Sticky, _____ bubble gum

Soft, _____ jelly

Hot, _____custard

Ripe, _____ banana.

Activity 10 – prompt sheet

Nightmare

It was a _____ night. I was walking next to some railway tracks. I

spotted my friend walking towards me across the track. He/she

looked_____. The silence was broken when suddenly, out of nowhere,

a _____ train sped up the track. My friend didn't seem to see or hear

the train and I _____.

It was too late. I watched in horror as he/she disappeared under the train. The

train screeched to a halt. I ran to my friend. I picked his/her body up and carried it

slowly towards the train. I was so angry and distraught.

I _____.

The driver smiled at me and opened the doors. I stepped onto the train. The driver

laughed as he closed the door and I suddenly felt a chill overcome me as I turned

around to see _____.

Activity 11

A play

In Tracy's nightmare everyone is against her.

⊃ Read the following play in which Tracy argues with everyone in the home and Mike tries to sort it out. This can be done as a class or in groups. It doesn't matter if the female roles are taken by males or vice-versa.

Character list (in order of the number of lines they have, largest first).
  Tracy
  Justine
  Mike
  Louise
  Peter
  Adele
  Jenny
(You could have a director reading out the lines in brackets.)

Scene: The lounge of the children's home.

(Tracy is sitting alone, writing in her book when Justine rushes in.)

Justine *(aggressively)*: What have you done with my photo, Tracy Beaker?

Tracy *(defensively)*: Which photo is that, Justine Littlewood?

(Mike comes in.)

Justine: You know what I'm talking about!

(Justine tries to grab Tracy and Mike steps between them.)

Mike: What's going on here?

Justine: She stole a photo of my dad!

Tracy: I did not. What would I do with a photo of your dad?

Justine: You're a liar, Tracy Beaker!

Mike: Calm down, Justine.

Tracy *(taunting)*: I suppose I could stick it on my door to scare people away. *(She laughs.)*

Mike: Stop it, Tracy. Now if both of you stop talking for a minute –

Justine *(spitefully)*: You're just jealous because I've got a dad.

Tracy: Why would I be jealous that you have that hairy-chested old ape for a dad?

Mike *(forcefully)*: Right. That's enough, Tracy. *(Turns to Justine who is crying.)* Sit down, Justine. I'm sure we can find your photograph. Don't worry.

(Peter and Louise have heard the row and come to see what's going on. Louise rushes to comfort Justine.)

Peter: What's the matter?

Mike: Justine's lost a photo of her dad.

Louise (to Mike): I've lost one of my dresses. I bet Tracy took that as well.

Tracy: Shut up, Louise. You look awful in it anyway!

Louise: Aha! How do you know which dress it was?

Justine (triumphantly): Yes. That's right. How would you know unless you took it?

Tracy: Louise looks awful in all her clothes.

Mike: Tracy! Everyone sit down and stop talking and we can try and sort this out. (When everyone is sitting down quietly.) Now, Justine. Where was the photo?

Justine: It was on the pinboard in my room.

Peter: Maybe it just fell off.

Tracy: Yeh. It's probably just fallen off and here you are, all accusing me, as usual.

Peter: I'm not accusing you, Tracy.

Tracy: Oh great. I'll be all right if I've got weedy Peter on my side, won't I?

Mike: Don't be so horrible, Tracy.

Louise: Yeh. Don't be horrible. (To Peter.) Peter, didn't you lose some pens a few days ago?

Peter (quietly): Yes . . . all my felt pens.

Justine: I bet Tracy took them as well.

Tracy (indignantly): I couldn't have taken them because someone scribbled on the noticeboard on my door in felt pen. I wouldn't scribble on my own notice would I? So either you did it, Peter, and hid the evidence, (to Louise and Justine) or one of you two stole his pens.

Justine and Louse: We didn't take them.

Mike: Let's just sort this photograph out. (To Justine.) Have you looked all over your room for it?

Justine: Yes. It's not there. Tracy's taken it. First she broke my clock and now she's taken my photograph.

Tracy: I didn't break your clock.

Louise: We know you did, Tracy, just like we know you've taken the photo, my dress and Peter's pens.

Tracy: What do you think I'd do with them? (Sarcastically) I could have a great evening in my room, couldn't I? Putting on Louise's dress and colouring a photo of Justine's dad with Peter's pens!

Justine: If you've touched my photo I'll kill you, Tracy.

Mike: Calm down, Justine.

(Just then Adele walks in.)

Adele: Has anyone seen my cherry-red lipstick? It's my favourite and I can't find it.

Louise: Tracy's probably taken it. She's taken loads of other things.

Tracy: I HAVE NOT. I HATE YOU ALL.

(At this point, Jenny walks in. She's holding the photo of Justine's dad.)

Jenny: I nearly put this in the washing machine, Justine. *(Giving her the photo.)* It was in with your dirty clothes. It must have fallen off your pinboard.

Justine *(stunned)*: Thanks.

Tracy: See, you all blamed me. I told you I didn't take it. You should have believed me. I bet you're all sorry now!

Peter: I believed you Tracy and I know you didn't take my pens.

Adele: I didn't say you took my lipstick, Tracy. I said it was missing. I'll go and look for it again. *(She leaves. Justine and Louise walk towards the door.)*

Louise *(mumbling)*: I still reckon she's got my dress.

Jenny: That's enough, Louise. Off you go.

Mike: I'm glad it's all been resolved. *(To Tracy.)* Maybe people won't be so quick to accuse you next time.

(Everyone leaves and Tracy is alone. She takes out the cherry-red lipstick and smiles.)

Extension activity

Find a space and act out the play concentrating on the directions. There should be no physical contact at all. When you've rehearsed it several times, perhaps you could present it to the class.

Note: The director wouldn't be reading the lines this time but organising the rehearsals instead.

Activity 12

Report on Tracy Beaker

Read pages 59 (second paragraph) – 63.

Tracy is disgusted by the advert Elaine placed in the paper about her.

⟳ Imagine you are Tracy's social worker. Write a longer report on Tracy in *four* paragraphs, for potential foster parents. You need to be *honest* but *positive* about her. Issues to consider include:

☆ Personal details, including age, what she likes to do; (p. 7 – 9 and p. 19)

☆ Family background and history in care. What is known about mother and father and mother's boyfriend, details of sequence of foster families and children's homes; (p. 14 – 17)

☆ Attitudes and behaviour. How did she get on at Aunty Peggy's and Julie and Ted's houses? (p. 16 and p. 25 – 26)

How does she behave with Elaine? (p. 26 – 30)

How does she behave with Jenny and Mike? (p. 33, p. 37 – 38, p. 40, p. 43 – 44 and p. 52)

In general, how well does she get on with the other children in care? You will have to include the incident with baby Steve and the ghost game at her foster home (p. 49 – 50), but you can also mention how she was with baby Camilla at her first children's home; (p. 11)

Does she have fits of temper? (p. 25)

How honest is she? (p. 25 and p. 44)

☆ What sort of parents you think are needed.

Extension activity

Now imagine *you* are Tracy and re-write the report using the same four paragraph subjects, changing the less positive parts.

Note: Remember to use Tracy's terminology.

TRACY

Tracy is lively, healthy, chatty, ten-year-old who has been in care for a number of years. Consequently she has a few behaviour problems and needs firm loving handling in a long-term foster home.

Activity 12 – prompt sheet

Report on Tracy Beaker

Note: Looking at pages 7 – 13 and 19 will help you with the first paragraph.

☆ Tracy is _____ years old. She has _____ hair. She likes

eating _____. Her favourite game is _____. She likes to

watch _____ films on television and her favourite subjects at school are

_____.

Note: Looking at page 16 will help you fill this second paragraph.

☆ Her family background is that her mother left and Tracy went first to a foster

family but _____

_____.

Then she went to a children's home but _____

_____

and is now in her second children's home where she is doing quite well.

Note: Fill in the gaps in the last two paragraphs from your knowledge of Tracy.

☆ Tracy's attitude towards other children is not what it should be. She is quite

aggressive and dishonest. She needs to learn to _____

_____.

☆ Tracy's attitude towards adults is not what it should be. She does listen when she

is spoken to but doesn't always think carefully about it or tell the truth. She needs

to learn to _____

_____.

☆ The sort of parents needed for Tracy are people who _____

_____.

Activity 13

Looks

Read pages 63 (first paragraph) – 74.

Tracy is very concerned to look her best for the writer. She thinks her mum is very attractive and seems to think that looks are very important.

Some people will spend a lot of money on plastic surgery and/or fashionable clothes in order to improve their looks.

⊃ Answer the following questions in sentences to form four paragraphs on this issue. You could discuss it first as a class or with a partner.

☆ Are you happy with the way you look?

> If you could change something about your appearance, what would it be?

> Would you consider plastic surgery?

> How much would you be prepared to pay for the treatment?

☆ Do you think people should be allowed to have non-essential plastic surgery on the NHS, given that funds are limited?

☆ List these personal qualities from most important to least important:

> hardworking
> healthy
> intelligent
> good looking
> well dressed
> trustworthy
> fun loving
> good sense of humour
> caring
> any others you think are important

☆ Do you think that people become obsessed with their looks because of the images of beauty that surround us or because of something in their personality? What do you suggest could be done about this?

Extension activity

Write a letter to an advertising company making the point that only a very small percentage of the female population are size 12 or below and that it is hurtful to many women to feel they are nothing like the 'ideal woman'. Similarly, it is hurtful to many men who do not have the perfect physique. Perhaps you should also point out that in using models who are 'good looking' – as defined by a few very particular characteristics – they are encouraging feelings of inadequacy. Another point you could mention is that people can do themselves serious physical and mental damage by striving to achieve the 'perfect look'. You could suggest how they could help to rectify the situation.

Activity 13 – prompt sheet

Looks

I am/am not happy with the way I look.

If I could change something about my appearance it would be

_____

_____.

I would/wouldn't consider plastic surgery because

_____

_____.

I do/do not think that people should be allowed to have non-essential plastic

surgery on the NHS.

Join these qualities a person could be judged on to their order of importance:

most important *	* hard working
second most important *	* healthy
third most important *	* intelligent
fourth most important *	* good looking
fifth most important *	* well dressed
sixth most important *	* trustworthy
seventh most important *	* fun loving
eighth most important *	* good sense of humour
least important *	* caring

I think that people become obsessed with their looks because

_____

_____

_____

Activity 14

Suitable clothes?

Read page 70.

Tracy says that Cam "... didn't look a bit like a *proper* writer". She obviously expects people in various professions to look a certain way. I think it's true that there is a *look* that is expected in certain jobs. I have to admit that, when I went into a school to talk to the pupils about my writing, I dressed as I thought they would expect a writer to dress. If the Prime Minister spoke on television dressed in a pair of baggy trousers, a leather jacket and a nose ring, it would raise a few eyebrows. People think that the way you dress says a lot about you.

Describe the sort of clothes you would *expect* a man or woman in these jobs to wear, and then invent a more 'eyebrow-raising' outfit for them:

☆ male manager
☆ female chef
☆ male racing driver
☆ female judge
☆ male navy officer
☆ female diver

Extension activity

Primary school teachers don't have to wear a uniform. Design or describe uniforms for male and female teachers in summer *and* winter, thinking carefully about both materials and the tasks a primary school teacher has to perform. They have to teach physical education, carry things like a whistle, pen and notebook, and may be working with messy things like paint, plaster or clay.

Activity 14 – prompt sheet

Suitable clothes?

I think a male manager would be expected to wear _____.

A more eyebrow-raising outfit would be _____.

I think a female chef would be expected to wear _____.

A more eyebrow-raising outfit would be _____.

I think a male racing driver would be expected to wear _____.

A more eyebrow-raising outfit would be _____.

A female judge would be expected to wear _____.

A more eyebrow-raising outfit would be _____.

A male navy officer would be expected to wear _____.

A more eyebrow-raising outfit would be _____.

A female diver would be expected to wear _____.

A more eyebrow-raising outfit would be _____.

Some clothes you may want to choose from for the expected outfits:

trouser suit; tie; smart shoes; skirt suit; blouse; long apron; chef's hat; white shirt and trousers; dark blue trouser uniform; white shirt; naval hat; smart, heavy shoes; long black gown; wig; white shirt; overalls; helmet; wetsuit; flippers; oxygen tank.

For the eyebrow-raising outfits you may want to choose from the above clothes, or some of the following clothes:

baggy trousers; leather trousers and jacket; shorts; trunks; tracksuit; riding trousers; jeans; camouflage trousers and jacket; long skirt; mini skirt; long dress; tee shirt dress; tee shirt saying . . .

Activity 15

Reading survey

Read pages 75 – 84.

On pages 75 and 76 Cam talks with the children about the kind of books they like. Adele loves ". . . all those soppy love books . . .", Maxy liked *Where the Wild Things Are* and Peter's nan used to like Catherine Cookson books.

⊃ Design a survey about the sort of things different people like to read in their spare time. Start by discussing as a class the sorts of things people like to read. As well as different types of books, don't forget other reading material such as newspapers, magazines, comics, etc. In Japan, reading comics is a favourite pastime for both men and women. Issues you could investigate include whether it is true that men and women prefer to read different things, whether women read more than men and whether your reading habits change as you get older.

You may want to consider the following questions:

☆ Which of the following do you read?
☆ Which of the following do you read most?
☆ How many hours of your spare time do you spend reading a day or week?

Don't forget to include details such as gender and age, if they are appropriate for your investigation. You may also want to include an 'other' option on your survey.

Extension activity

Design a book to appeal to someone who doesn't like reading. First think of the topic for the book, then design a front and back cover. Next design each page, labelling any parts necessary. Try to add features such as pop-ups, lift flaps, noise features, fold outs, etc.

Activity 15 – prompt sheet

Reading survey

Ask a number of people to answer the following questions:

Which of these types of reading material do you read most?

☆ adventure/mystery stories
☆ ghost/horror stories
☆ animal stories
☆ factual books
☆ comics
☆ magazines (including television listings)
☆ newspapers
☆ other

You could mark each person's response with a tally mark. Remember to cross through the bunch on the fifth tally. Be careful not to ask the same person twice. A list of names may be useful.

When you have collected all your responses, plot the results of your survey on the bar chart below. Think carefully about your scale.

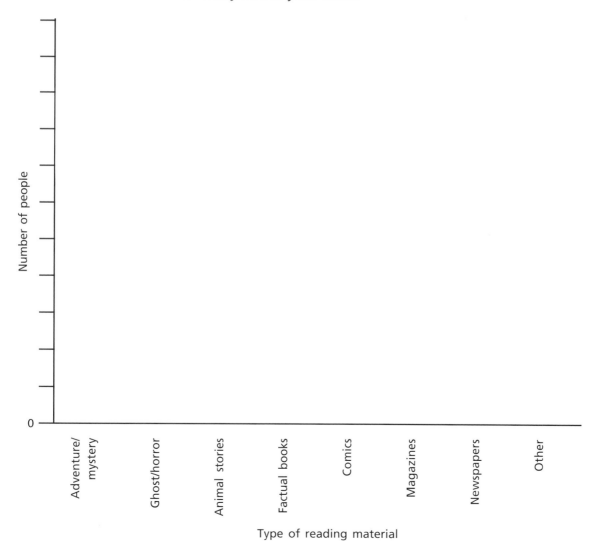

Activity 16

Throwing a wobbly

Read pages 80 – 82.

Tracy throws a 'wobbly' and gets sent to the Quiet Room.

Have you ever just gone mad for a while? What was it that wound you up? What did you do? Write about it. Try not to be too negative about people and/or change names.

Note that you have probably written (as most fiction is written) in the past tense: "I <u>went</u> mad once when I . . ." It has happened already and is in the past.

Are there some 'shocking' things you think you may *yet* do? Write about them. I may yet get up on the stage at the theatre, before the show starts, and sing a 'little number'. I may also stand up on a bus or train packed full of people and tell them to cheer up and enjoy every moment of their life because it is so precious and can be so short!

Note that you are writing in the future tense: "I may yet . . ." These things are yet to happen. They are in the future.

Extension activity

Imagine you are an anger management counsellor. How would you try to help Tracy? List the questions you would ask her; what you would say to her, and/or any role-play ideas. You may find it useful to research this topic first. Look in your library or ask your teacher if there is any appropriate reading available to staff that you could look at.

Activity 16 – prompt sheet

Throwing a wobbly

I haven't ever gone mad/I once went mad when _____

_____

I may yet do the following 'shocking' things:

I may _____

_____

I may _____

_____

I may _____

_____

I may _____

_____

Activity 17

Dares

Read pages 85 – 97.

You learn more about the relationship between Tracy, Justine and Louise. Tracy and Justine dared each other to do various things.

⊃ Make a list of realistic dares or forfeits that could be used at a party of people your age.

⊃ Which ones would you *least* like to do?

Extension activity

Imagine being dared by someone to do something that was dangerous and being called a chicken for not wanting to do it. Peer pressure is hard to resist. How could you respond? You could include things like: "Not doing that only means I'm not daft . . . You can think what you like . . . I'm not risking getting hurt just to keep you amused . . ." etc.

Activity 17 – prompt sheet

Dares

Here is a list of dares or forfeits that could be used at a party:

(You might want to think up some nasty mixes of food to eat; things to balance on various body parts; things to try to do in a certain length of time; things to do with your teeth or feet that you normally do with your hands, or things to do blindfolded.)

_____

_____

_____

_____

_____

_____

_____

Here is the order in which I would *least* like to do them with the *worst* one first:

_____

_____

_____

_____

_____

_____

_____

Activity 18

Handwriting

Read pages 98 – 108.

Tracy's letters to Cam are printed whereas Cam's handwritten letters are cursive, i.e. joined.

⊃ Copy Tracy's letter on page 106 in your best handwriting.

⊃ How neat do you think your handwriting is in comparison to Tracy's and Cam's?

Everyone has different handwriting styles but there are some rules that should be followed. Look at what you have written and answer these questions:

☆ Do the tops of your capitals and tall letters ('t', 'd', 'f', 'h', 'k', 'l', 'b') touch or come close to the top of the writing line? (They should.)

☆ Are your small letters half the size of, or noticeably smaller than, your capital and tall letters? (They should be.)

☆ Do the tails of your 'g', 'j', 'p', 'q', 'y' and possibly 'f' go under the writing line? (They should.)

☆ Have you joined your capitals? (You shouldn't. Depending on your style, you may not join your 'x' and 'z', but all other small letters should be joined.)

⊃ Now get together with a partner. Decide who will write first. The other person is watching the writer to see how they do in terms of these handwriting rules: every letter should be easily recognisable, e.g. the 'u' should not look like a 'v'. You should write each letter consistently, e.g. every 'a' should be identical to every other 'a'.

The watcher must concentrate, as the writer copies the following sentence in his or her neatest handwriting, joining if possible:

Is this easy to read and do I write my letters the same way every time?

☆ The watcher should now tell the writer how he or she did.

Now do the same task for the following rules:

Each word should be written in one easy, flowing, continuous movement with the dots of the 'i' and 'j', and the crossing of the 't', being done at the *end* of the word.

Try this sentence:

Are my words written in one movement or do I keep taking my pen off the paper?

The last rule is: you should begin most of your letters at the top and end at the bottom.

Try this sentence:

Do I write most of my letters from top to bottom?

Now swap over, so that the watcher becomes the writer and the writer becomes the watcher. Do the above exercise again.

Extension activity

Choose a book and begin copying from the text in your neatest handwriting, forming the letters as you have been practising and remembering the rules you have been taught.

Activity 19

An alternative fairy tale

Read pages 109 – 123.

In Tracy's letters to Cam she introduces Goblinda the Goblin, a character unlike the traditional fairy-tale characters.

Several writers have written these sorts of alternative fairy stories, including Tony Robinson in *There's a Wolf in my Pudding*. This is a collection of rewrites of traditional fairy tales. Some of them are retold from the point of view of the baddie. For example, in *There's a Wolf in my Pudding*, the big bad wolf tells us of his unjust treatment in the traditional fairy tale. He argues that in fact he was a skinny, kind wolf, that he was only after Little Red Riding Hood's picnic basket and that she and her gran cooked up the story between them in order to cover up his murder.

⊃ Write an alternative fairy tale for children aged ten and over. You can base it on a well-known tale or make one up. Write on alternate lines so re-drafting will be easier. Take time to plan your story first.

Extension activity

Work with a partner to re-draft your story. Concentrate on the following points:

☆ You need a gripping or humorous opening line;
☆ Each part of the story needs to be clear;
☆ The story needs to flow rather than be disjointed;
☆ Your story should be dramatic and/or humorous;
☆ There should be at least two characters;
☆ The characters should be described well enough for your reader to picture them;
☆ There should be speech throughout the story;
☆ The characters' personalities and motives should come through in their speech and actions;
☆ Throughout your story you should use adjectives to improve your descriptions;
☆ Check your punctuation including full stops, commas, speech marks and paragraphing;
☆ Check your grammar.

Activity 19 – prompt sheet

An alternative fairy tale

Here is an idea and a story start for a rewrite of the fairy tale *The Three Little Pigs*:

The wolf claims that he had a really bad cough and cold and that he was trying to ask the pigs if they had any medicine that would help. He knocked on the straw house first, asking for help, but no-one opened the door. Then he sneezed and the house blew down. Next he went to the stick house, but unfortunately coughed and it fell down. Finally he went to the brick house, but this time, when no-one answered, he thought the only way to get in and see if they had some medicine was to climb down the chimney. To his horror, those nasty little pigs boiled him in a pot of water. Now he's thinking of taking them to court over it.

Finish this story in your own words:

I am not a big bad wolf at all. I was, on that day, a poor unwell wolf. I had a dreadful cough and cold. I had heard that there were three nice pigs living nearby and I believed they might help me. I thought they might have some medicine I could have. How wrong I was! I went to the first little pig's straw house.

_____

_____

_____

_____

_____

_____

_____

_____

_____

_____

_____

_____

Activity 20

Bullying

Read pages 113 and 114.

Tracy is shocked that Cam thinks she is bullying Peter and talks about a bully in her first home.

⊃ Read the beginning of this story about bullying:

It was Tuesday and Ajay needed to get home quickly, so his dad could go to work. He always had to look after his baby sister on a Tuesday.

"See you tomorrow," shouted his mate James, as he got on the bus.

As Ajay walked quickly down the street, he realised that there was a group of older lads behind him who seemed to be catching him up. He tried to ignore them, but it wasn't long before they were right on his heels.

"You're in a hurry. Did we scare you? Poor little thing," one of the lads said in Ajay's ear. They started laughing. Ajay tried to ignore them and kept on walking.

"Hey Mick, I don't think he heard you," said one of the other lads.

They were coming up to an alley on the right, when Mick grabbed Ajay by the arm and pushed him into it. He swung Ajay round to face him and the other lads formed a circle around them. Ajay was trying not to look frightened. He didn't recognise any of them but they obviously went to his school, because of their uniforms. There were six of them and they were all staring at him.

"Look, I've got to get home," he said, and tried to step past Mick, who blocked his way.

"Why are you in such a hurry?" asked Mick. Ajay tried to look past him out of the alley. Mick took Ajay by the shoulders. "I asked you a question," he said angrily.

"Look, I've got to go," he said quietly, trying not to look at Mick.

"Don't you like our company? What are you saying? Do we smell or something?" asked Mick.

"No. Look, I've got to babysit my sister," said Ajay quickly. All the lads started laughing.

"That's nice, isn't it?" sneered Mick. "What a nice boy! Being nice won't get you anywhere, you know. We'll have to toughen you up." They stopped laughing. Mick suddenly hit Ajay in the stomach. "There's your first lesson in life. No need to thank me. I'll give you the odd lesson now and again just so you don't forget," he said, as Ajay crumpled to the ground, in pain.

When Ajay eventually got to his feet, the boys had gone.

⊃ What do you think Ajay should do now? Discuss the options open to him as a class. These might include telling someone; trying to avoid the bullies; facing up to the bullies, or trying to reason with Mick when he is on his own.

⊃ Now finish the story choosing one of these options. The story can end as you think it would in reality, or as you think it *should*.

Extension activity

Write down a few ideas you could put forward if you were asked to set up an anti-bullying policy in your school. You may find it helpful to do some research on the subject. Try to find some literature in the library, or ask your teacher if there is any appropriate reading available to staff that you could look at.

You might want to think about the following things:

* Establishing ground rules to allow all pupils to 'live together';
* Having individual chats with both bullies and the bullied, and/or bringing them together;
* Getting the bully, and perhaps the bullied, to sign an agreement about behaviour in the future;
* Organising follow-up sessions;
* Taking the problem to a group of pupils who will act as a bullying council;
* Putting the bullied and the bullies, and perhaps all pupils in the school, through some assertiveness sessions, looking at things such as: telling people how you feel and what you want; responding to name-calling; how to leave a bullying situation; and how to feel better about yourself.

Activity 20 – prompt sheet

Bullying

Here are a few ideas for each of the options open to Ajay, and a story start:

☆ If he decides to tell his parents they might go to the school and/or Mick's parents;

☆ If he decides to tell his teacher they would want to talk to Mick and may want to talk to Ajay and Mick together. They may call Mick's parents in;

☆ If he decides to tell his friend James, he may want to get their friends together and face the bullies, but this might lead to more trouble. James might advise Ajay to tell his parents or teacher, or to stand up to Mick when he's on his own;

☆ If he decides to avoid the bullies, he could stay away from school or pretend to be ill. But this might get him into more trouble. Perhaps he could keep going to school, taking care not to bump into them;

☆ If he faces up to the bullies on his own, they may respect him for it. He would need to think carefully about what he was going to say and do beforehand. Perhaps this might get him into more trouble;

☆ If Ajay is going to try to catch Mick on his own and try to reason with him, he would have to think carefully, beforehand, about where he should best do this, and what he is going to say and do.

Bully story ending:

Ajay spent the evening in his room, thinking about the problem. He finally decided that the best way to handle the bullying was to

_____

_____

_____

_____

_____

_____

_____

_____

_____

Activity 21

First day nerves

Read pages 124 – 136.

On pages 127 – 132 a new girl arrives at the home. Imagine how she must feel. Remember what Justine was like when she first arrived at the home (p. 85 – 90).

Most people can vividly remember their first day at a new place because we tend to be a bit nervous about it. Think of your first few days at primary school, your first date, moving to a new house, or some other situation which was memorable.

⊃ Now write about this. Try to describe the events, the surroundings, the other people and your feelings, as well as you can. The best pieces of writing allow the reader to picture things vividly in his or her mind. For example, if you read the following two pieces of writing about a teacher, Mr Bowman, coming into a classroom, you can see the difference.

He was called Mr Bowman. He was tall, he was ugly. He sat on his table. He had glasses.

Mr Bowman strode into the room. I'd never seen anyone so huge. When he stood in front of you he blocked out everything else and all you could do was pray you hadn't done anything wrong. He was very ugly, but you would never let him hear you say it. There were thick, dark hairs growing out of his nose and ears. His squashed nose looked like it had been broken several times. It made us wonder what sort of person could have broken it. He sat down on his table with a thump and glared at us over his thick-framed spectacles.

Note: Writing on alternate lines will make it easier to re-draft.

Extension activity

Re-draft your piece of writing, concentrating on adjectives and adverbs.

Do this short exercise on adverbs, which describe the verbs in italics, to remind you what they are.

Adverbs tell you more about the verb (action). In the following text, underline the adverbs. The first two have been done for you. Find the other ten.

The boy *thought* <u>long</u> and <u>hard</u> about it. He had to do something. He *sprang* suddenly to his feet and *sprinted* quickly back home. He was *breathing* heavily when he reached the house. He *thumped* furiously on the door and when it opened he *strode* purposefully through it, *burst* confidently into the lounge and *stood* squarely in front of his big sister.

"I want you to stop singing in the bath. You've got a terrible singing voice and it drives me mad!" he said, *staring* firmly at her. His sister was shocked that her weedy little brother could be standing up for himself.

"Okay," she *said* quietly.

He *walked* away contentedly.

Activity 21 – prompt sheet

First day nerves

Here are some descriptive words and phrases you may want to use in your writing:

☆ nervous

☆ scared

☆ frightened

☆ butterflies in my stomach

☆ shaking

☆ trembling

☆ sweating

☆ amazement

☆ horror

☆ shock

☆ miserable

☆ I was lost

☆ I didn't want to look foolish

☆ I didn't know what I was doing

☆ everyone else seemed to know what to do

☆ everything seemed so big

☆ I felt so small

☆ I felt that I would never be confident about it

☆ I wished I was somewhere else

☆ I wished the day would just end

☆ the time seemed to go so slowly

Activity 22

Conflicts

Read pages 133 – 136.

Tracy has an argument with Justine and Elaine tries to sort it out. These two are always arguing, and Elaine, Jenny and Mike have a difficult job trying to stop them.

You may already know how difficult it is to try and intervene when two people are arguing.

⊃ Get into groups of three or four. You can take it in turns to play two people who are arguing and someone who tries to intervene. If there's a fourth person, they can take the role of an observer.

You need to decide what sort of things the two antagonists are arguing about.

Perhaps they are related or live together and are arguing over something to do with this, or perhaps they're strangers and have just crashed their cars.

Then you need to choose one of these situations and decide whether the person who is going to intervene has a specific role, e.g. police officer or just a passer-by.

The observer needs to concentrate on the strategies used by the person intervening and decide how effective they are. It is important that you do not get carried away with this. There should be little or no physical contact between actors, and remember that you are only acting!

⊃ When you have done one piece of improvisation you should listen to your observer (if you have one) and then discuss how it went and how you felt while you were role-playing. Concentrate on the strategies used by the person intervening. Which ones worked best?

⊃ Swap roles and/or situation a few times.

Extension activity

Prepare a short report for the class, briefly stating your chosen situation and then outlining the strategies the intervener used. Discuss which ones you found worked well and which did not.

Activity 22 – prompt sheet

Conflicts

Here are some more ideas for situations of conflict and an improvisation start for one situation:

Three people live in a house together. Two of them wash the bathroom and kitchen and vacuum more than the third. The third person argues that he or she isn't in the house as much of the time and so shouldn't have to do as much cleaning. This person feels that the first person should always clean the bathroom because he or she is in there all the time. The first person isn't happy about this and the second person is trying to intervene.

One person lends a bike to a friend, asking for it to be put away in the garage when it is finished with. The friend uses the bike but leaves it lying on the drive because the garage isn't open. The first person then gets into the car, reverses down the drive and drives straight over the bike, mangling the front of it. A third person who is a mutual friend tries to intervene.

A person falls in love with a best friend's partner and the partner feels the same way. The best friend and the partner had only been going out together for a short time and were having problems. The pair meet in secret a few times and decide to tell the third person, but they are spotted before they have a chance to come clean.

Improvisation start for a car accident:

Jo: What on earth were you doing?
Sam: What do you mean? It was you who was daydreaming.
Jo: I wasn't daydreaming, I was checking what was behind me in the mirror. It's called good driving!
Sam: Yes . . . but I was in front of you.
Jo: Yes and you suddenly put your brakes on for no reason, which is what caused the accident.
Sam: There was a bird.
Jo: Rubbish. I didn't see a bird.
Sam: Well it must have been a leaf being blown across the road.
Jo: A leaf! You made us crash for a leaf? That's just great. You need glasses mate and anyway you're not supposed to stop for animals.
Sam: Try telling that to the bird.
Jo: There wasn't a bird.
Sam: Well, anyway, if you hadn't been checking your look in the mirror, you'd have had time to put your brakes on.
(A policeman arrives after some time . . .)
Policeman: What's going on here then?

Activity 23

Sequence the story

Read from page 137 to the end of the book.

⟳ Put these events in Tracy's life in the correct order and write them out to form a summary of Tracy's life history. *Leave two lines between each event* in case you do the Extension activity. Reading page 16 again will help you.

Tracy is fostered by Julie and Ted.

Tracy makes friends with Louise at her second children's home.

Peter meets a couple who want to foster him.

Tracy is fostered by Aunty Peggy.

Tracy meets Cam.

Justine arrives at her second children's home.

Tracy's mum, whom she adores, leaves her.

Tracy makes up with Justine.

Tracy goes to her first children's home and meets baby Camilla.

Tracy falls out with Justine and Louise.

Extension activity

In the space you've left between each event, add a comment on it *from Tracy*. For instance, underneath 'Tracy is fostered by Aunty Peggy' you could write 'What a silly old smacking machine she was' on Tracy's behalf. Remember to use speech marks and Tracy's terminology.

Activity 23 – prompt sheet

Sequence the story

Cut out these ten events in Tracy's life along the dotted lines and stick them in order, one below the other with the latest last.

. . . .

Tracy is fostered by Julie and Ted.

. . . .

Tracy makes friends with Louise at her second children's home.

. . . .

Peter meets a couple who want to foster him.

. . . .

Tracy is fostered by Aunty Peggy.

. . . .

Tracy meets Cam.

. . . .

Justine arrives at her second children's home.

. . . .

Tracy's mum, whom she adores, leaves her.

. . . .

Tracy makes up with Justine.

. . . .

Tracy goes to her first children's home and meets baby Camilla.

. . . .

Tracy falls out with Justine and Louise.

. . . .

Part 2: Activities for the whole book

Activity 24

Continuing The Story of Tracy Beaker

⊃ Write a short play continuing the story.

You could set the first scene in Cam's car. Imagine that Cam has taken Tracy out for the day and has just brought her back to the home. While they are talking in the car outside, Tracy pushes Cam for a decision about fostering her. Cam informs Tracy of her decision.

A second scene could be set in the dining room of the children's home where everyone is eating dinner. Tracy could rush in and be asked how she enjoyed the day. How will she react to this?

Look back at the play in Activity 11 to help you.

Extension activity

Get together with one or two friends and choose which play you would like to use. Then rehearse it. Remember that there must not be any physical contact and think about how the character is feeling when he or she is speaking.

Activity 24 – prompt sheet

Continuing The Story of Tracy Beaker

Scene: *In Cam's car. Tracy and Cam have just come back from a day out.*

Tracy *(smiling her biggest smile)*: Cam, have you decided yet whether you can foster me? I know I've been horrible sometimes, but I will be nice forever if you foster me.

Cam *(taking a deep breath)*: _____.

Tracy: _____.

Scene: *In the dining room. All the children are eating. They look up as Tracy comes in.*

Justine: Did you have a good day?

Tracy: _____.

_____

_____

_____

_____

_____

_____

_____

_____

_____

_____

_____

_____

_____

Activity 25

Crossword

CLUES ACROSS

1. Tracy Beaker is writing a book about her life story. This is called an __. (p. 107)

2. What is the name of the fairy-tale character that Tracy develops in a letter to Cam? (p. 109)

3. What did Tracy call the doll that her mum bought for her when she was in her first home? (p. 38)

4. What is Tracy's favourite number? (p. 10)

5. What did Tracy find in Cam's flat to write with? (p. 149)

6. Tracy wants to be fostered by a fantastic, rich __. (p. 10)

7. How old is Tracy? (p. 7)

8. Tracy isn't happy about having to share her __ with Peter Ingham. (p. 7)

9. Who are the two people who look after the children at the home? (p. 43)

10. Tracy describes Cam's __ as '. . . weeny . . . and ever so shabby'. (p. 148)

11. If Tracy gets a Rottweiler dog all her __ had better watch out! (p. 12)

12. Who lives at the children's home, is 16, has a Saturday job at BHS and has a drawer full of make-up? (p. 64)

13. Tracy admits to __ sometimes. She says Aunty Peggy used to call it telling fairy stories. (p. 25)

14. What is one of the only things that Tracy doesn't like eating, especially when it has '. . . great fatty lumps in it' – Aunty Peggy used to make her eat it all up. (p. 13)

15. Who wrote *The Story of Tracy Beaker*?

16. Tracy's favourite game is playing with __. (p. 12)

CLUES DOWN

1. Who does Tracy refer to as '. . . that silly old smacking machine . . .'? (p. 51)

2. Tracy thinks she is really __. She thinks she gets a hundred out of a hundred nearly every time she does a test. (p. 31)

3. Tracy thinks her mum may be in __ because she '. . . looks so great she'd easily get into the movies'. (p. 87)

4. Peter Ingham meets this couple who want to foster him – note the unusual spelling. (p. 155)

5. What are Tracy's favourite sorts of TV programmes? (p. 13)

6. Tracy quite fancies being a __ so she could make up evil spells. (p. 8)

7. When Tracy sneaks down to the kitchen for a midnight feast she tries to blame her raid on the fridge on a mountaineering __. (p. 52)

8. Is Tracy's hair dark or fair? (p. 9)

9. When Cam comes to the home the second time she says it is to __ Tracy. (p. 115)

10. Aunty Peggy used to make Tracy milk pudding. It had '. . . little, slimy, bubbly bits . . .' in it. What did Tracy tell the other kids that these bits were? (p. 34)

11. Tracy __ Justine to eat a worm. (p. 91)

12. Julie wasn't Tracy's idea of a glamorous foster-mum. She wore __. (p. 46)

13. Tracy likes helping in the __ because she can pinch food when Jenny turns her back. (p. 33)

14. Who used to be Tracy's best friend? (p. 34)

15. *The Story of Tracy Beaker* is illustrated by __ Sharratt.

Extension activity

Do the prompt sheet crossword as well.

Crossword Grid

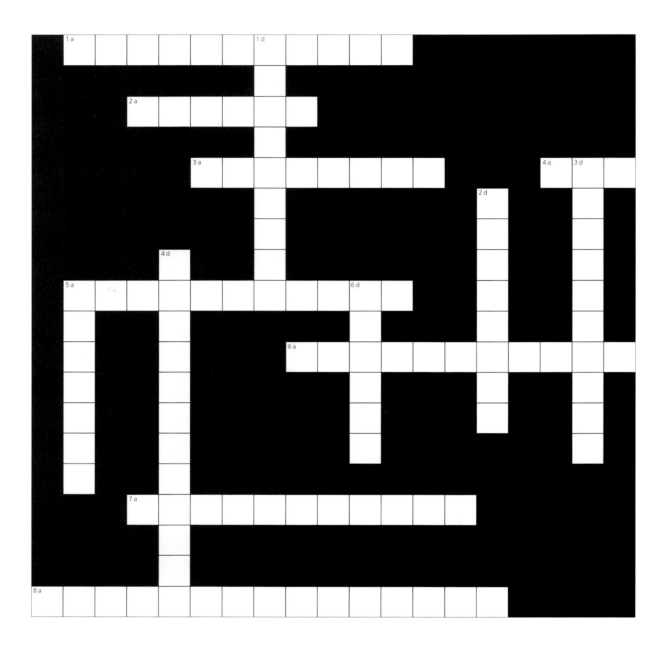

Activity 25 – prompt sheet

Clues across

1.

2.

3.

4.

5.

6.

7.

8.

Clues down

1.

2.

3.

5.

4.

6.

Crossword Grid

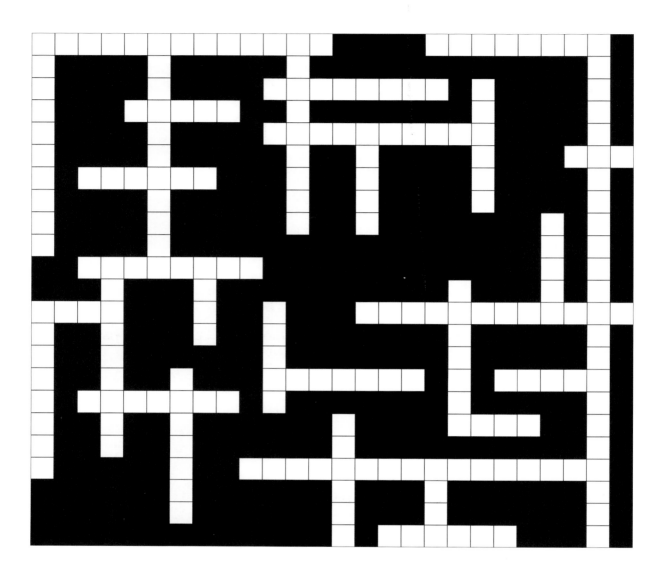

Activity 26

Design your own crossword

⊃ Design your own crossword from the book.

Here are some words to help you:

☆ childrenshome
☆ fosterfamily
☆ mickeymouseclock
☆ elaine
☆ nightmares
☆ magazine
☆ midnightfeast
☆ birthdaycake
☆ mcdonalds
☆ camsflat
☆ taperecorder

It's easier to plan a crossword on large, squared paper.

It also helps if you start with a long word across the top or down the side and then try and link other long words from it to spread out in both directions.

Some of the words are linked below as an example:

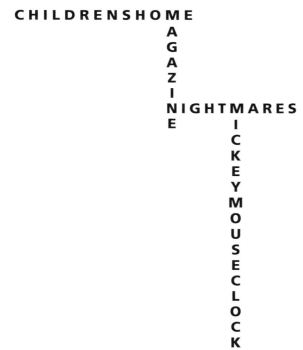

Extension activity

Now copy your crossword grid onto squared paper, being very careful about the number and position of the squares and colouring in the squares that haven't any letters in them. Remember to number and label your clues.

A further Extension activity could be to scramble the words you have used, i.e. change the order of letters and ask a friend to try to unscramble them. Could he or she do it without any clues?

Activity 27

Spelling sheets

Here are five lists of words that appear in the book and five matching lists of sentences containing those words. Thus the words are being read and, when testing, can be written in context.

The first few words on each list have a spelling rule in common.

Choose a list appropriate to the pupil: if ten words are too many to learn then give them a few from the list.

Lists A contain the more common, everyday words. Lists B contain more unusual words. Lists C contain the most complex words.

Further notes on the spellings and activity ideas

Another way to check the pupils' understanding of the words, apart from reading them out within a sentence, is to get them to write out their own sentence for each word.

I have found (and teachers seem to agree) that one of the best ways of learning spellings is by look, cover, write and check. This literally means look at the word carefully and think about the sounds, then cover the word and attempt to write it from memory. Next, uncover your attempt and check it against the original. I tend to say to the pupils that they have to get it right five times.

Spelling list 1

A	B	C
difficult	annoying	usually
discuss	fibbing	sorrowful
feeling	hopeless	disappointing
guess	useless	eventually
address	suppose	intelligence
kitchen	swollen	mountaineering
ignore	assumed	accounting
surprise	fault	hilarious
waiting	favourite	enemies
talking	expect	measuring

The first few words on each list contain double letters.

A

"You can be DIFFICULT to handle, Tracy Beaker," said Elaine.

"We'll DISCUSS this later," said Cam.

"I'm FEELING very angry.""You'll never GUESS what. Peter Ingham thinks I'm his best friend!"

"My mum didn't leave a forwarding ADDRESS."

"I like to help in the KITCHEN."

"Justine has scribbled in my book. IGNORE it."

"It would be a brilliant SURPRISE if my mum turned up."

"I spent all morning WAITING for Cam."

"I wasn't TALKING to you, Justine."

B

"I like to be ANNOYING and not do what I'm asked."

"I'm not FIBBING," said Justine."Peter Ingham is HOPELESS at writing."

"My paint brushes are USELESS now."

"School's okay I SUPPOSE."

"Justine's nose is all SWOLLEN where I hit her."

"Jenny ASSUMED I broke Justine's clock."

"I lost my second placement through no FAULT of my own."

"My FAVOURITE game is playing with make-up."

"I EXPECT I'll be moving on soon."

C
"Jenny's ploys and tricks don't USUALLY work on me."

"I think you do care," said Jenny in a silly SORROWFUL voice.

"It was DISAPPOINTING when I realised the letter was not from my mum."

"Cam arrived EVENTUALLY. I had waited forever."

"I've done heaps of INTELLIGENCE tests."

"It would take a MOUNTAINEERING mouse to get into the fridge."

"There's no ACCOUNTING for taste."

"The boy looked HILARIOUS when he stepped in his custard-filled boots."

"I've tried MEASURING my height with a ruler."

"I'm going to get a big dog and then my ENEMIES had better watch out."

Extension

Find as many words in the dictionary as you can with double consonants in them. Try to spot patterns.

Spelling list 2

A	B	C
angry	typical	absolutely
anyone	naughty	sympathetically
family	mystery	hysterics
friendly	probably	seriously
crying	recently	autobiography
lovely	actually	responsibility
lying	imagine	necessarily
anyway	private	gorgeous
money	rescue	glamorous
suddenly	apologise	decency

The first few words on each list contain a 'y' which makes an 'I' or 'E' sound.

A

"Sometimes I get really ANGRY."

"I don't want ANYONE to see my book."

"I want to be fostered by a rich FAMILY."

"A rabbit can't give you a FRIENDLY lick like a dog."

"I'm not CRYING. I've got something in my eye."

"There was a LOVELY baby called Camilla at my other home."

"You're LYING Tracy Beaker," screamed Justine.

"I don't want to do it and ANYWAY it's stupid."

"They give you MONEY if you foster someone."

"I SUDDENLY felt hot as I opened the letter. It could be from my mum."

B

"That's TYPICAL. Someone has spoilt this page in my book."

Aunt Peggy would say, "Oh Tracy, you NAUGHTY girl."

"We didn't find out who did it. It was a MYSTERY."

"My mum will PROBABLY come and get me soon."

"I haven't had a lot of letters RECENTLY."

"Mike talked about rules and RESPONSIBILITY."

"IMAGINE a Mars Bar as big as a bed."

"This is my PRIVATE book."

"I went to RESCUE Elaine from boring little Peter."

"Jenny wants me to APOLOGISE to Justine."

C
"I'm just joking. I would ABSOLUTELY hate you to foster me, Elaine."

"Elaine sighed SYMPATHETICALLY."

"Louise and Justine were still having HYSTERICS at my appearance."

"Peter Ingham is writing so SERIOUSLY in his book."

"I stamp and scream a lot ACTUALLY."

"I'm writing my AUTOBIOGRAPHY."

"It's not NECESSARILY a fib."

"You only live happily ever after if you're a goodie-goodie and you look GORGEOUS."

"I tried to make myself look GLAMOROUS."

"I knew Justine was still listening. Some people have no DECENCY at all."

Spelling list 3

A	B	C
allowed	believed	borrowed
laughed	fostered	advertised
smiled	decided	concerned
shouted	insisted	experienced
tried	managed	convinced
quite	sighed	complained
quiet	organised	worried
because	nervous	disqualified
notice	couple	impression
questions	slightest	

The first few words in each list end in 'ed', which often denotes past tense, at the end of a verb.

A

"We weren't ALLOWED to take toys to school."

"Elaine LAUGHED when I said she was trying to be super-cool."

"Elaine SMILED at me.""Justine and I SHOUTED at each other."

"I've TRIED measuring how tall I am but the ruler wobbles."

"My nose is QUITE sore where Justine hit me."

"I've been sent to the QUIET room."

"My mum keeps moving BECAUSE she gets fed up living in one place for too long."

"I've put a NOTICE on my door to keep people out."

"Normally adults you meet ask stupid endless QUESTIONS."

B

"The other kids BELIEVED me when I told them there were fish eyes in the pudding."

"I want to be FOSTERED by a nice rich family.""I DECIDED not to go out in case my

mum came to get me."

"I INSISTED Jenny was wrong."

"My mum hasn't MANAGED to come and see me yet."

"Elaine SIGHED when she read the bit about Aunty Peggy."

"It would take some ORGANISED searching to find my mum."

"I was NERVOUS about meeting Cam."

"Julie and Ted were a nice COUPLE."

"I wasn't the SLIGHTEST bit sorry."

C
"I once BORROWED make-up from Adele."

"They've ADVERTISED me in the paper now."

"As far as I'm CONCERNED, I'm good with babies."

"I'm really EXPERIENCED when it comes to babies."

"I had CONVINCED myself Justine wouldn't stoop so low."

"I COMPLAINED at first when Justine used to hang around with us."

"I SUSPECTED Jenny was coming so I cleared off."

"I'm not WORRIED about it."

"Louise and Justine said I was DISQUALIFIED in the dare game but I wasn't."

"I needed to make a good IMPRESSION on this writer woman."

Spelling list 4

A	B	C
dumb	wriggling	typewriter
know	whisper	whining
honest	knock	whopping
write	listened	gnawing
wrong	answers	whinged
whole	cupboard	fidgeting
found	boring	placement
though	straight	appearance
thought	direction	allowances
through	awful	behaviour

The first few words in each list contain a silent letter.

A

"Justine's dad took her on some DUMB outing."

"I don't KNOW when I started this book."

"It would be fun fostering me, HONEST it would."

"I love to WRITE in my book."

"I wanted Julie and Ted to keep me but it all went WRONG."

"I'd like a WHOLE birthday cake to myself."

"I never FOUND out who hurt my doll."

"It's funny THOUGH, I used to use this toy telephone."

"I never THOUGHT anyone would stoop so low."

"I looked THROUGH the make-up in Adele's room."

B

"I hope frogs and toads come WRIGGLING out of Aunty Peggy's mouth every time she speaks."

"Don't worry Peter – just WHISPER to Jenny and she'll sort it out."

"I still get excited when there's a KNOCK at the door."

"Aunty Peggy never LISTENED to me."

"They don't tell you the ANSWERS in the intelligence tests."

"I shut baby Steve in a CUPBOARD."

"Louise was a bit BORING. She wouldn't muck around with the make-up."

"Justine said I spat the worms out STRAIGHT away, but I didn't."

"I flicked a cornflake in Justine's DIRECTION."

"Aunty Peggy was an AWFUL cook."

C
"Cam does her stories on a TYPEWRITER."

"Peter Ingham is always WHINING to Jenny."

"No-one's ever grateful even when you do them a WHOPPING great favour."

"Imagine GNAWING away at the corner of a giant Mars Bar."

"Mike WHINGED on about rules and responsibility."

"Cam kept FIDGETING with her pen."

"I know it was hard when your second PLACEMENT went wrong," said Elaine.

"Justine's famous dad put in an APPEARANCE at last."

"Elaine wanted to clip me round the ear but she was making ALLOWANCES for me."

"I've got BEHAVIOUR problems."

Extension

Investigate rules for silent 'w', 'h', 'g' and 'k'. Find silent letter words and underline them.

Spelling list 5

A	B	C
afternoon	advert	generally
everything	desperate	awkwardly
either	understand	certain
wonderful	murder	properly
other	interview	permanently
together	perfect	hideous
trouble	miserably	expression
would	expensive	incredible
careful	voice	suitable
hopeful	unfair	spoilt

The first few words in each list contain 'er'.

A

"Cam's coming this AFTERNOON."

"I like eating EVERYTHING."

"I don't know my weight. I don't know my height EITHER."

"Imagine that WONDERFUL chocolate smell."

"I don't want any of the OTHER children to help me."

"Peter and I have to cut our birthday cake TOGETHER."

"I didn't get into TROUBLE about my uniform but the kids stared at me."

"If I was a kitten I WOULD grow long claws and sharp teeth and scare everyone."

"I was CAREFUL not to bump into Jenny again."

"I was HOPEFUL I'd be adopted by now."

B

"Elaine put an ADVERT in the newspaper about me."

"I think they're getting DESPERATE to get me fostered."

"I can UNDERSTAND why you are angry with me, Tracy," said Elaine.

"I could MURDER a Mars Bar right this minute."

"Cam is going to INTERVIEW me for the magazine."

"You'll find the PERFECT placement one day," said Elaine.

"Peter Ingham is failing MISERABLY to write neatly in his book."

"The clock wasn't EXPENSIVE. It couldn't have cost much."

"Peter Ingham spoke with a squeaky VOICE."

"It's UNFAIR that Peter shares my birthday."

C
"When someone tells me to go away I GENERALLY stick to them like glue."

"Cam's hand reached out AWKWARDLY to touch Peter."

"I told Louise about a CERTAIN problem that I have at night."

"I haven't got the right stuff to do my art project PROPERLY."

"In my dream my friend asked me to stay at her house PERMANENTLY."

"Justine pulled a HIDEOUS face at me."

"That's a daft EXPRESSION. Why would I cut off my own nose to spite my face."

"I turned myself into an INCREDIBLE vampire with the make-up."

"Aren't you a SUITABLE fosterparent, Elaine ?"

"You can't leave anything around without it getting SPOILT."

Extension

Other ways to say 'er', i.e. 'ur' and 'ir'.

Activity 28

Tracy Beaker – my review

Look at the back cover of the book.
Read the review by *The Guardian* newspaper.

⊃ Do your own, more detailed review of this book. Use the title: 'Tracy Beaker - my review' and write a short paragraph, answering each of the questions below:

Where is the story set?
Who is/are the main character/s and what are they like?
What is your favourite part of the story?
What is your least favourite part?
Which parts of the story would you change?
How does the story end?
Would you recommend the story to a friend or not? Why?

Extension activity

Write some more book reviews of books you have read, using the same format.

Activity 28 – prompt sheet

Tracy Beaker – my review

The story is set

_____

The main character is a girl of ten called

_____

In the story she

_____

_____

My favourite part of the story is

_____

_____

The part of the story I like least is

_____

_____

I _____ recommend this story to a friend.

Activity 29

Target readers

Books tend to appeal more to certain types of reader (their **target** reader). Readers vary, for instance, in terms of age, and the sort of books they like.

The Story of Tracy Beaker would probably appeal to a fairly wide range of children: perhaps to children aged seven to fifteen, who enjoy humorous books with lots of illustrations.

⮑ Write the title 'Target readers' in your book and then do an analysis of this book, or another that you have read, by answering the following questions, *in full sentences*.

What is the title of the book?
Who is the author?
How many pages are there?
What is the book about?
Are the illustrations good – and are there plenty of them?
What sort of reader do you think would enjoy this book?

Extension activity

Do this target analysis for each of a range of books.

Activity 29 – prompt sheet

Target readers

The title of my chosen book is

_____

The author is

_____

It has _____ pages in it.

It is about

_____

_____

It _____ got a lot of good illustrations in it.

I think that the kind of people who would enjoy reading it are

_____

_____

_____

Activity 30

Comparing books by the same author

Look at the second of the introductory pages in *The Story of Tracy Beaker*. It lists other books by Jacqueline Wilson.

⊃ Do a comparison of books by the same author. Choose an author and at least two of their books. Write the title 'Comparing books by the same author' in your book and answer the questions below *in full sentences*.

What are the titles of the books?
Who is the author?
How are the books similar? (In terms of things like number of pages, layout, illustrations, characters, themes and endings.)
How do the books differ? (Use the above list again.)
Which book did you prefer and why?

Extension activity

Swap your work with others in the class. If they have chosen books and/or authors you are familiar with, did they have different opinions to you? If they chose books/ authors unfamiliar to you, perhaps you will get some ideas for other books that you might enjoy.

Activity 30 – prompt sheet

Comparing books by the same author

The titles of the books I've chosen to compare are

_____

_____

My chosen author is

_____

The books are similar in that

_____

_____

_____

The books are different in that

_____

_____

_____

My favourite of these books is

_____

because

_____

_____

Some useful words/phrases are: _characters, illustrations, themes, endings, number of pages._